magic
wand
fairy
black cat
spell
spell
broomstick
caldron
witch
wizard
castle
Gingerbread man
dragon
prince
princess

contents

Picture word book

compiled by LYNNE J BRADBURY
illustrated by LYNN N GRUNDY

This collection of words is about children and their environment. The book presents words children use, words they see around them and the words for objects with which they are familiar.

Each object or scene is illustrated using simple, bold, full color pictures. The book is arranged by subject and not alphabetically so that, for example, a child wanting the word kettle will find that word in the kitchen scene.

Very young children will enjoy talking about the pictures with an adult and having the objects named for them. Older children will be able to use the book as reference for their reading and writing as well as for enjoyment.

An alphabetical index is provided at the back of the book to assist the parent or teacher.

PRINTED IN BELGIUM

Girl Boy

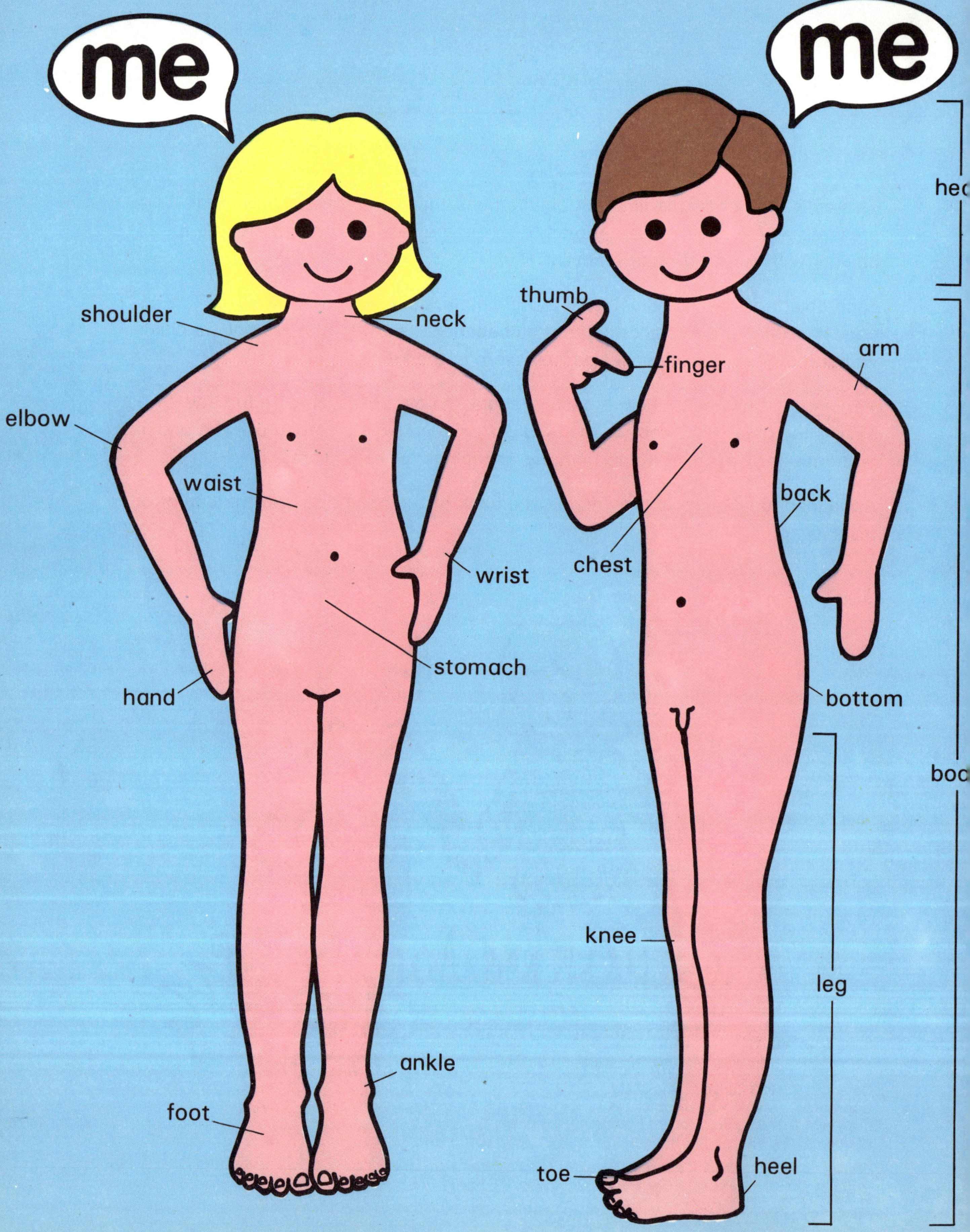

me
me
shoulder
neck
elbow
waist
wrist
stomach
hand
ankle
foot
thumb
finger
arm
back
chest
bottom
knee
leg
toe
heel

Face

hair
nose
chin
forehead
eyelash
lip
eye
cheek
mouth
eyebrow
ear
nostril

Clothes

indoor clothes

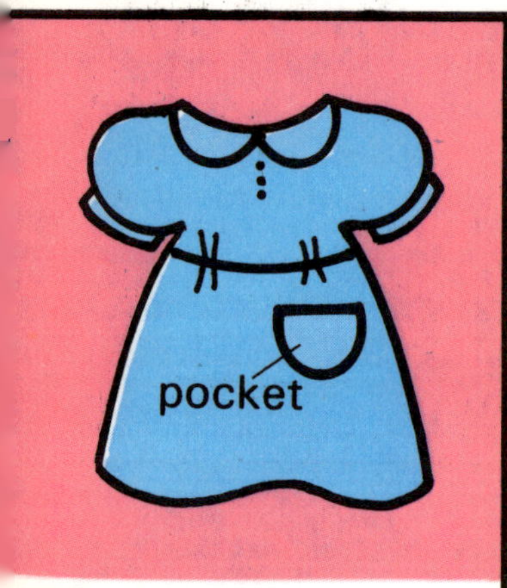

dress

sweater

socks

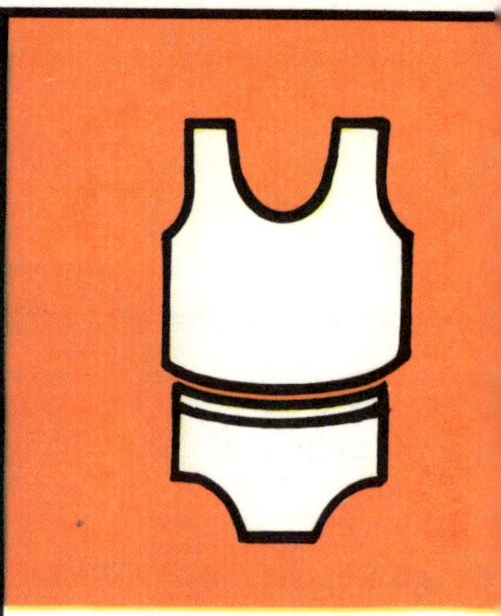
undershirt and briefs

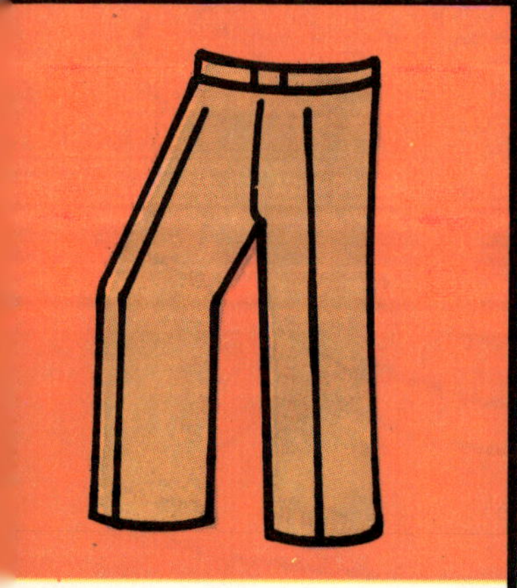
trousers

blazer/jacket

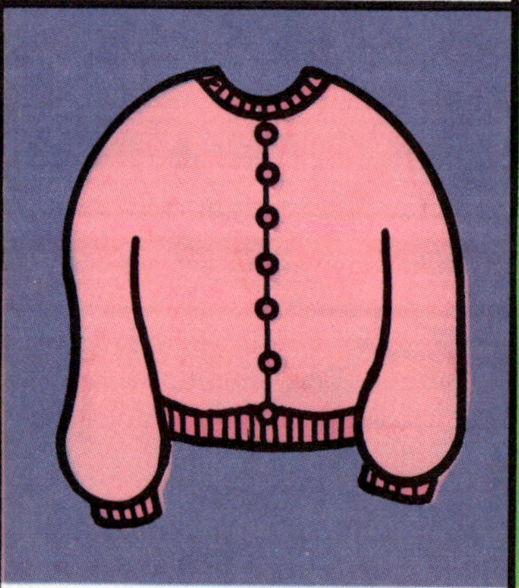
cardigan

tee shirt

outdoor clothes

hat

coat

boots

mackintosh/raincoat

shoes

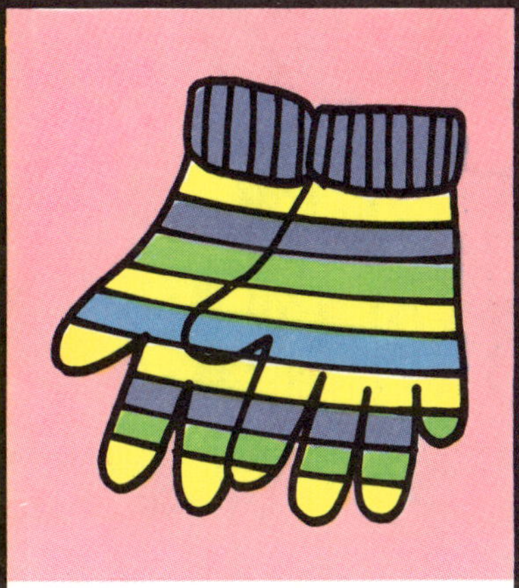

gloves

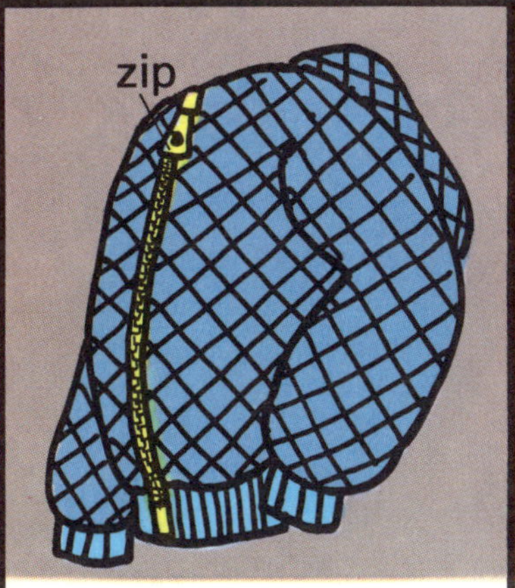

ski jacket

scarf

night clothes

Family

father/
dad/
daddy
aunt/
auntie
mother/
mom/
mommy
brother
baby
uncle

grandmother/
grandma/
granny/
nanna/
nanny
grandfather/
grandad/
grandpa
sister
cousin
brother

Home

apartments
chimney
house
roof
tiles
gutter
window
drainpipe
window
window sill
porch
bell
front door
keyhole
mailbox
step
gate
bricks
hedge
sidewalk

Living room

telephone
bookcase
radiator
ire-place
vase
record player
grate
stereo speaker
hearth
couch/ sofa/ settee
cushion
television
plant
rug
armchair
radio
lamp
ashtray
coffee table
carpet

Dining room

picture
teapot
cup
saucer
tray
fruit bowl
server
chair
fork
plate
water jug
knife
spoon
glass
table-mat
pepper
salt
tablecloth

Kitchen

patula
ladle
sieve
grill
spice rack
faucets
dish pan
draining board
pot
frying pan
sink
rawer
pboard
oven
dish towel
stove
rolling pin
iron
freezer
kettle
ug
mixer
refrigerator/ fridge
stool
trash can
vashing machine
dustpan
brush
vegetable rack

Bedroom

light
closet
coathanger
rail
mirror
comb
brush
dressing table
pillow
blanket
sheet
bed
bedspread
teddy bear
carpet
quilt
alarm clock
book
hot water bottle
bedside table

Bathroom

mirror
cabinet
shampoo
talcum powder
razor/ shaver
toothpaste
nail brush
shelf
faucets
toothbrush
towel
toilet
toilet paper
face cloth
sink
bubble bath
shower
sponge
soap
bath tub
bath mat
scales

Yard

bush
shed
clothes line/
washing line
hose
shovel
pitch-
fork
hoe
rake
swimming pool
watering can
ball
frog
plants
seed box
lawn
stones
seeds

tree
greenhouse
tree
swing
compost/rubbish heap
flower bed
wn mower
wheelbarrow
soil/ earth
vegetables
trowel
plant pots

Car

fence
garage
lawn
trash can
driveway
car seat
windshield
trunk
gas cap
steering wheel
hood
headlight
windshield wipers
door handle
turn signal
parking light
hub cap
door
license plate
tire
bumper
wheel
CAR 123

Tool shed

tool box
work bench
ladder
broom/brush
oil can
glue pot

file
chisel
screws
screwdriver
pliers
nails
plane
hammer
pincers
wrench
drill
electric drill
ax
saw

Park/Playground

kite
fence
rocking horse
swing
see-saw
slide
merry-go-round
pail
shovel
sandbox

Street

garage
tavern
sweetshop
The Green Apple
gas pump
trash can
motor cycle
town hall
fish shop
vegetable store
book shop
car
yellow line
road
bus
hardware shop
jeweler
supermarket
butcher
IN
OUT

multi-storey parking garage
hairdresser
shoe shop
electrical shop
florist
stoplight
truck
white line
crosswalk
movie theater
post office
drugstore
café
1
2
3
vement
Police
mailbox
police car
bank
clinic/ health center
policewoman
telephone booth
traffic lights
crosswalk
oliceman

Supermarket

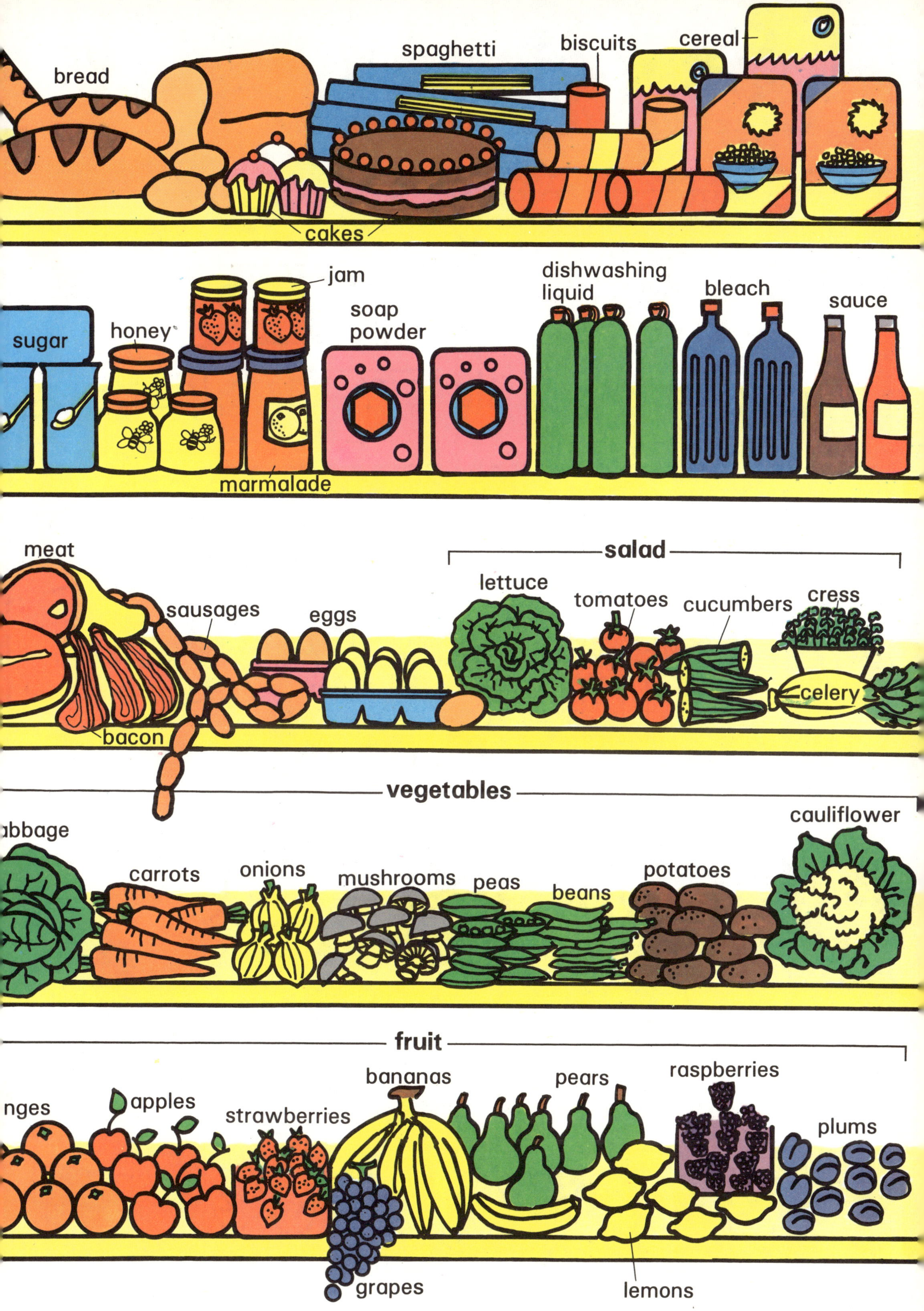
bread
spaghetti
biscuits
cereal
cakes
jam
sugar
honey
soap powder
dishwashing liquid
bleach
sauce
marmalade
meat
salad
lettuce
sausages
eggs
tomatoes
cucumbers
cress
celery
bacon
vegetables
abbage
carrots
onions
mushrooms
peas
beans
potatoes
cauliflower
fruit
nges
apples
strawberries
bananas
pears
raspberries
plums
grapes
lemons

School

clock
monkey bars
playground
book corner
milk bottles
girl reading
ball
gym apparatus
boy singing
hoop
beanbag
skipping rope
children dancing

blackboard
pictures
2 -
3 -
mathematics/sums/
number
register
sk
pen
ruler
teacher
chalk
waste
paper
basket
painting
paintbrush
building
blocks
pencil
paper
scissors
abcdef
writing
crayons
drawing
jigsaw
glue

Hospital

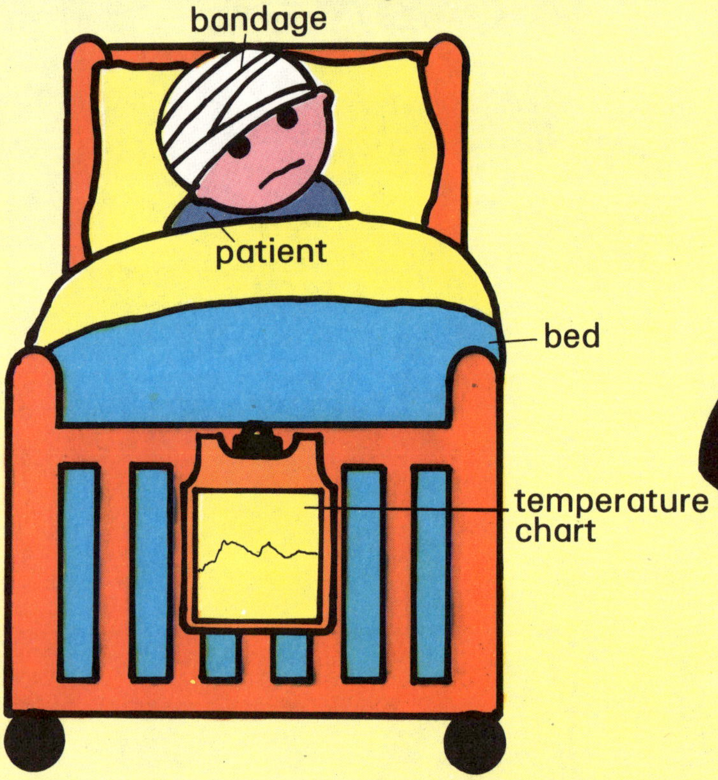

doctor nurse

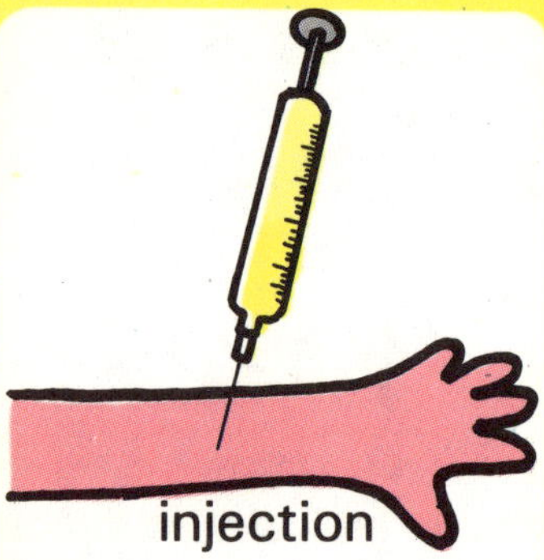

injection

ambulance

wheel-chair

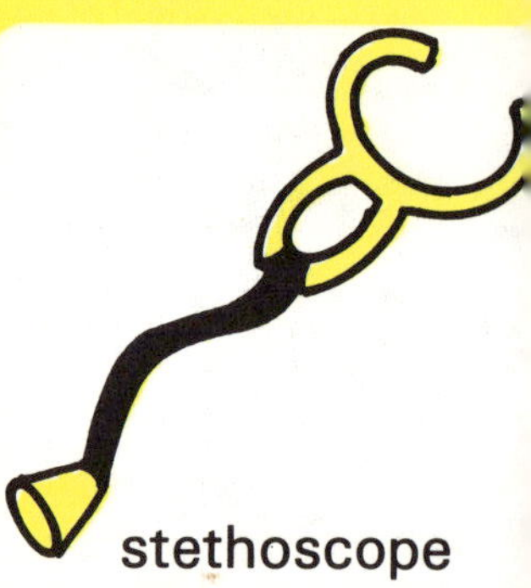

stethoscope

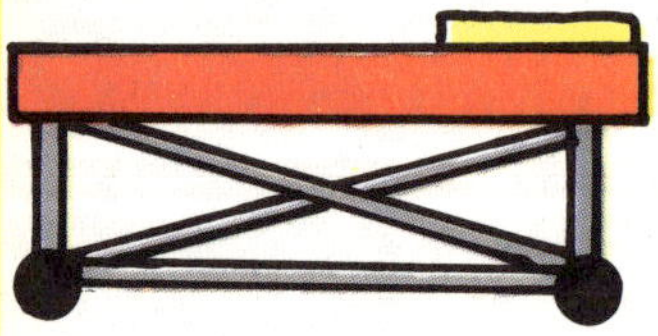

operating table

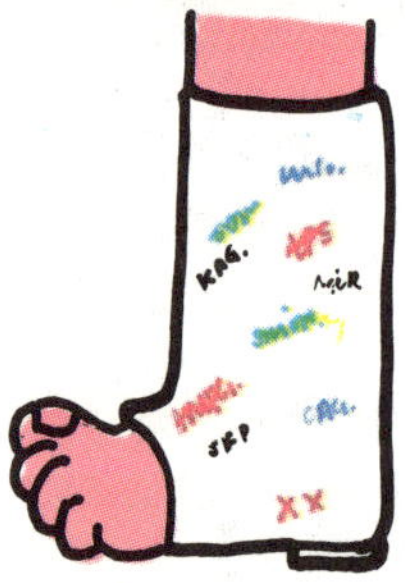

cast

thermometer

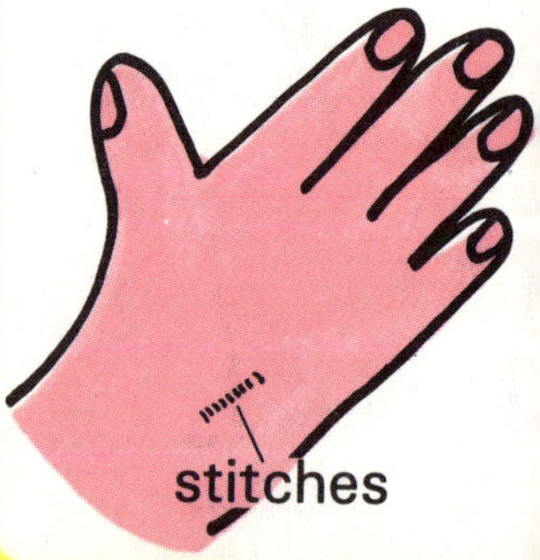

stitches

operating room

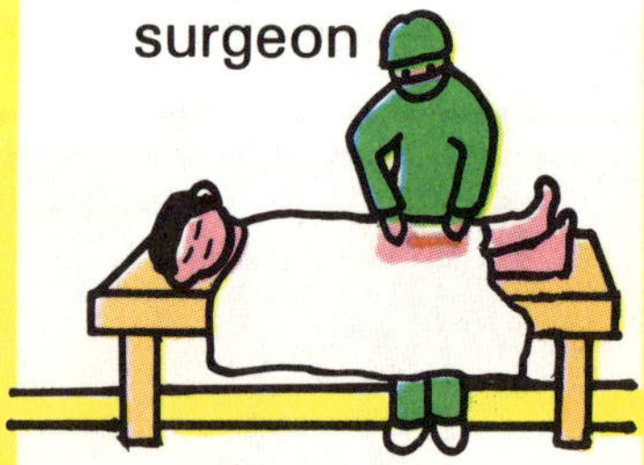

operation

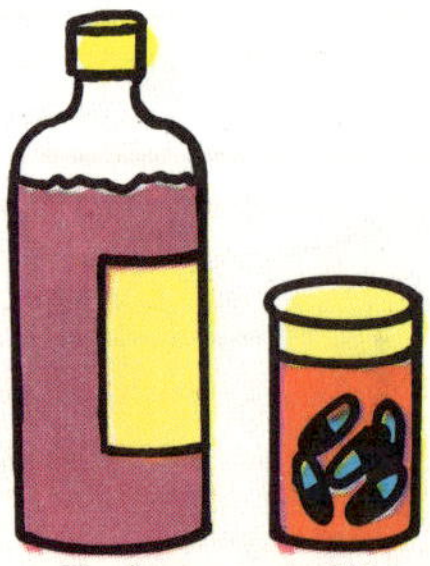

medicine pills

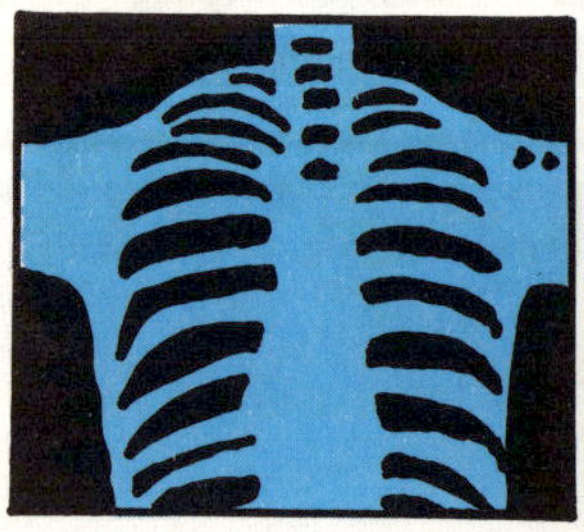

x-ray

Dentist

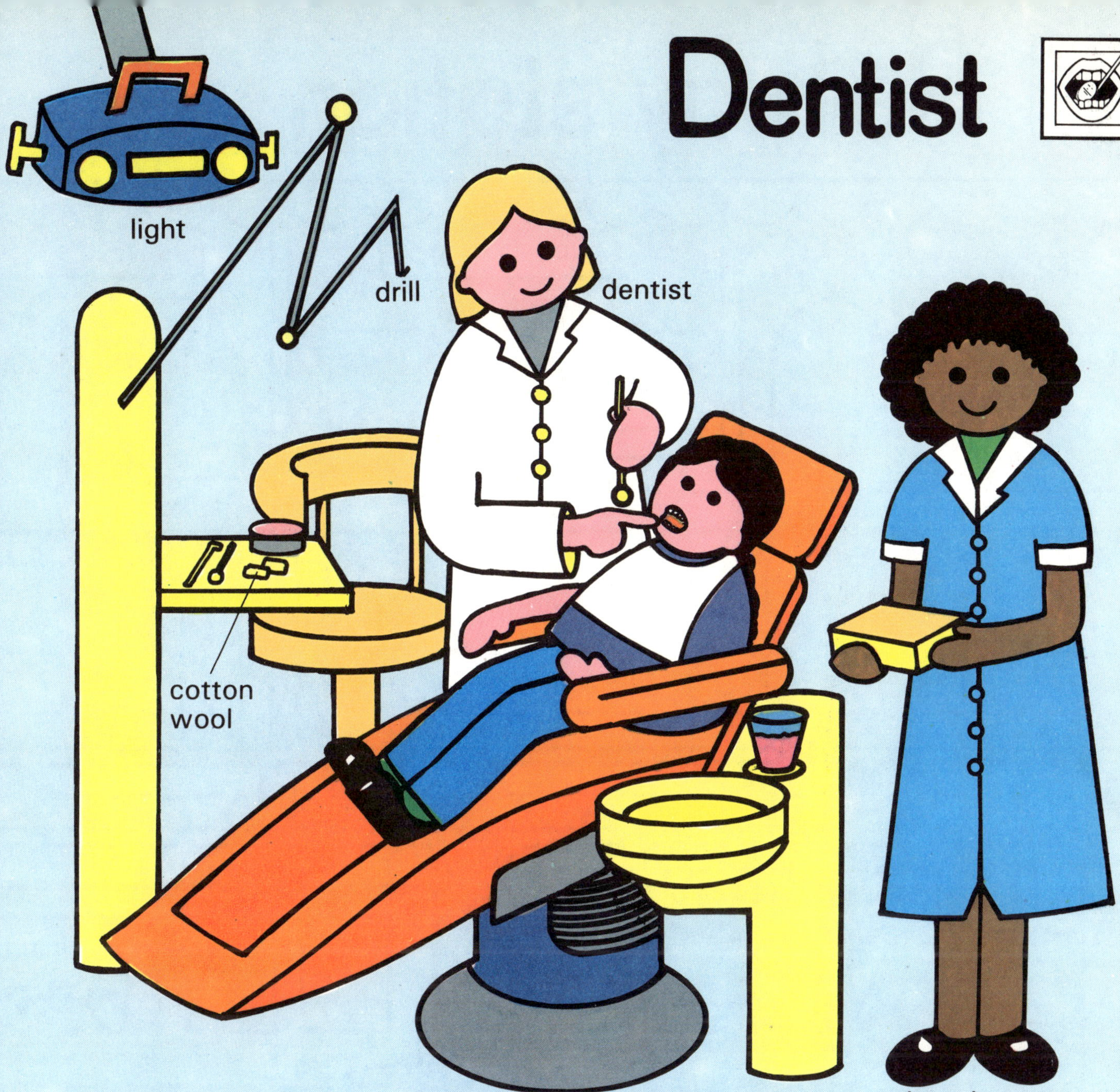

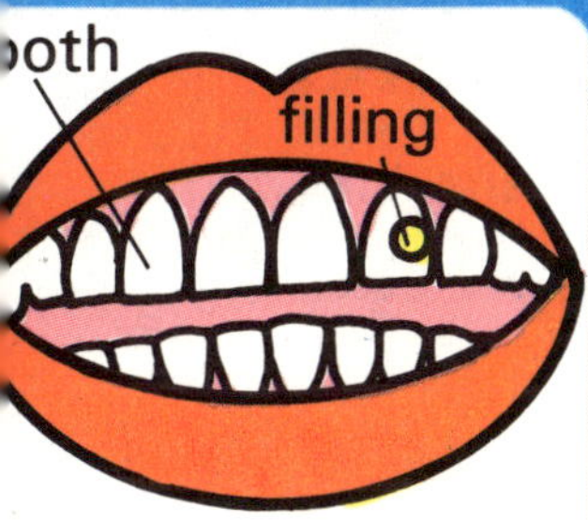

teeth

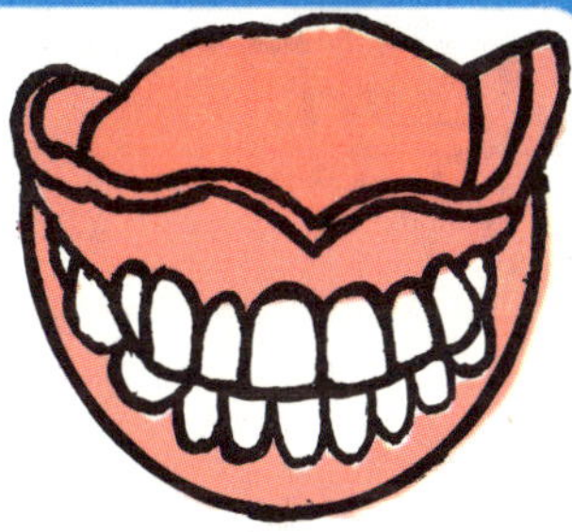
false teeth

mouthwash

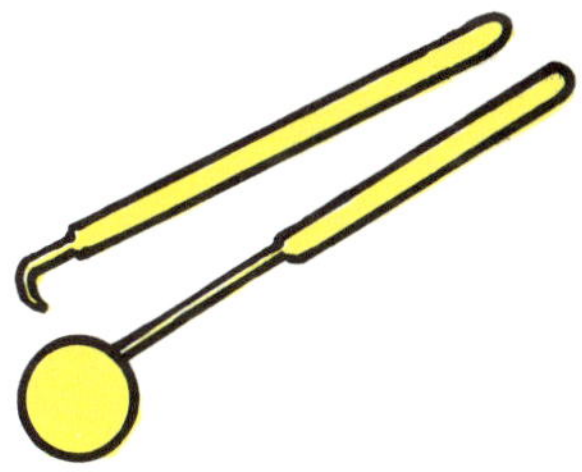
instruments

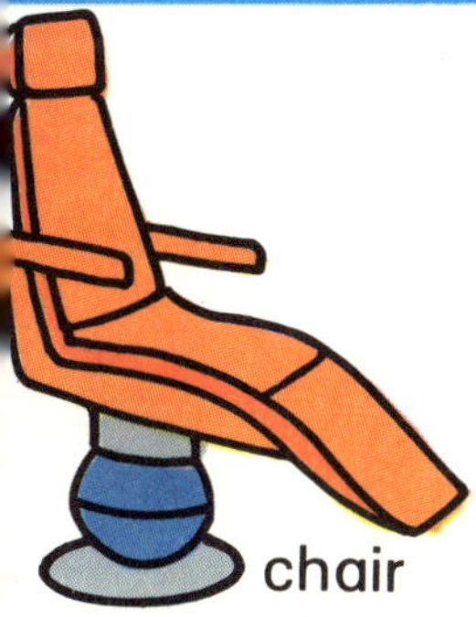
chair

waiting room

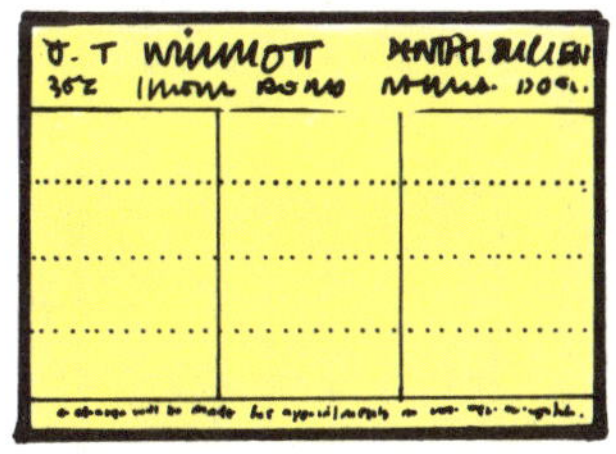
appointment card

receptionist

Railway station

Bus station

ticket office
snack bar
ticket
conductor
wheel
bus
bus stop
single-decker bus
pay as you enter
driver
bus fare
handbag
briefcase
basket
passengers

Docks

lighthouse
barge
smoke stack
tugboat
cabin
deck
ship
harbor
tanker
mast
cargo
cargo ship
crane
rope
anchor
sailor
captain
dock

Airport

wing
airplane
control tower
helicopter
unway
customs
ockpit
fuselage
tail
steps
pipe
fuel tanker
air stewardess
air steward
pilot
mechanic
radar scanner

Countryside

highway
hedge
nest
field
scarecrow
tractor
plough
bridge
bull
goat
river
tree
cow
calf
stile

Seashore

seagull
umbrella
wind break
deck chair
beach bag
air bed
sunglasses
beach ball
towel
swimming trunks
bathing suit
rubber rin
rock
rock pool
crab
seaweed

icecream truck
sun
donkey rides
steps
boardwalk
shovel
donkey
bikini
sandcastle
bucket
beach
wave
shell
starfish
shrimp
sea
fish
lobster
pebbles

Zoo

cage
monkey
lion
hippopotamus
parrot
elephant
crocodile
polar bear
seal
zoo keeper

tiger
snake
kangaroo
zebra
rhinoceros
giraffe
dolphin
elican
penguin

Amusement Park

ferris wheel
slide
side-shows
coconut shy
rifle range
bumper cars
cotton candy
candy apple
popcorn

Circus

band
trapeze
trapeze artist
acrobat
lion
strongman
circus ring
seal
ringmaster

Big Top/circus tent
tightrope walker
performing dogs
audience
elephant
ballerina
ggling
horse
clown

Musical instruments

trumpet

tuba

french horn

flute

recorder

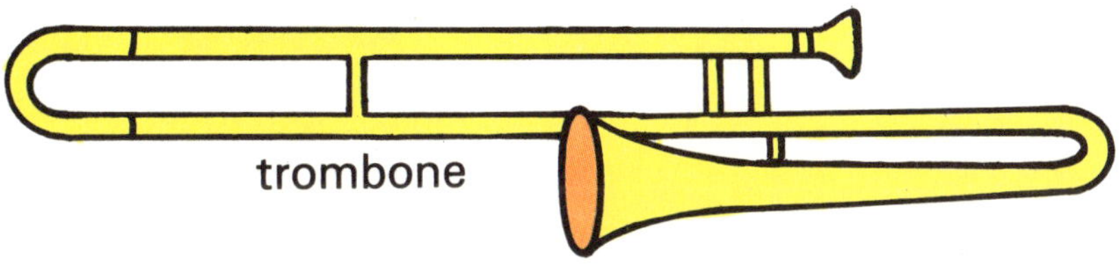
trombone

drum

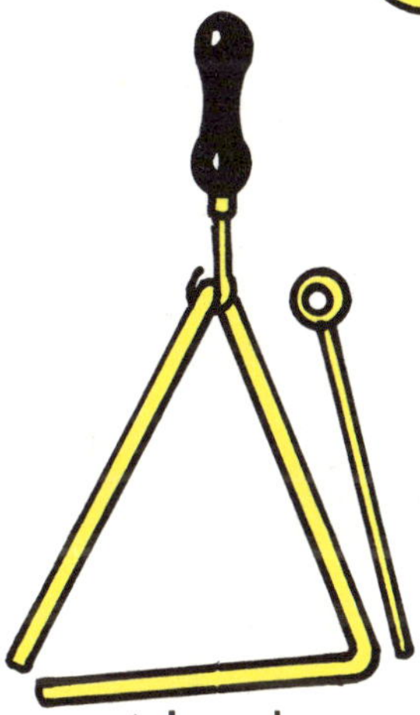
triangle

bongo drum

castanets

cymbals

tambourine

xylophone

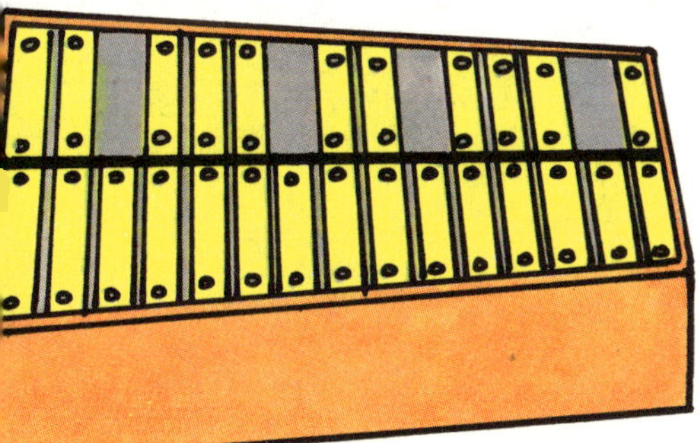
glockenspiel

Jobs

chef/cook

waiter/waitress

engineer

garbage man

teacher

milkman

miner

hairdresser

factory worker

salesperson

fireman

truck driver

doctor

nurse

postman/postwoman

butcher

policeman/policewoman

scientist

Sports

swimming

cricket

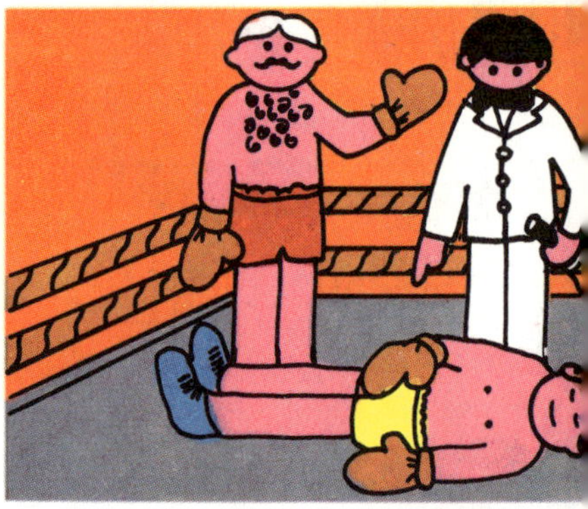

boxing

motor racing

skiing

golf

tennis

sailing

ice skating

show jumping

soccer

fishing

motor cycle racing

wrestling

rowing

running

badminton

hang gliding

rugby

basketball

pool

wind surfing

hurdling

cycling

parachuting

hockey

table tennis

Small creatures

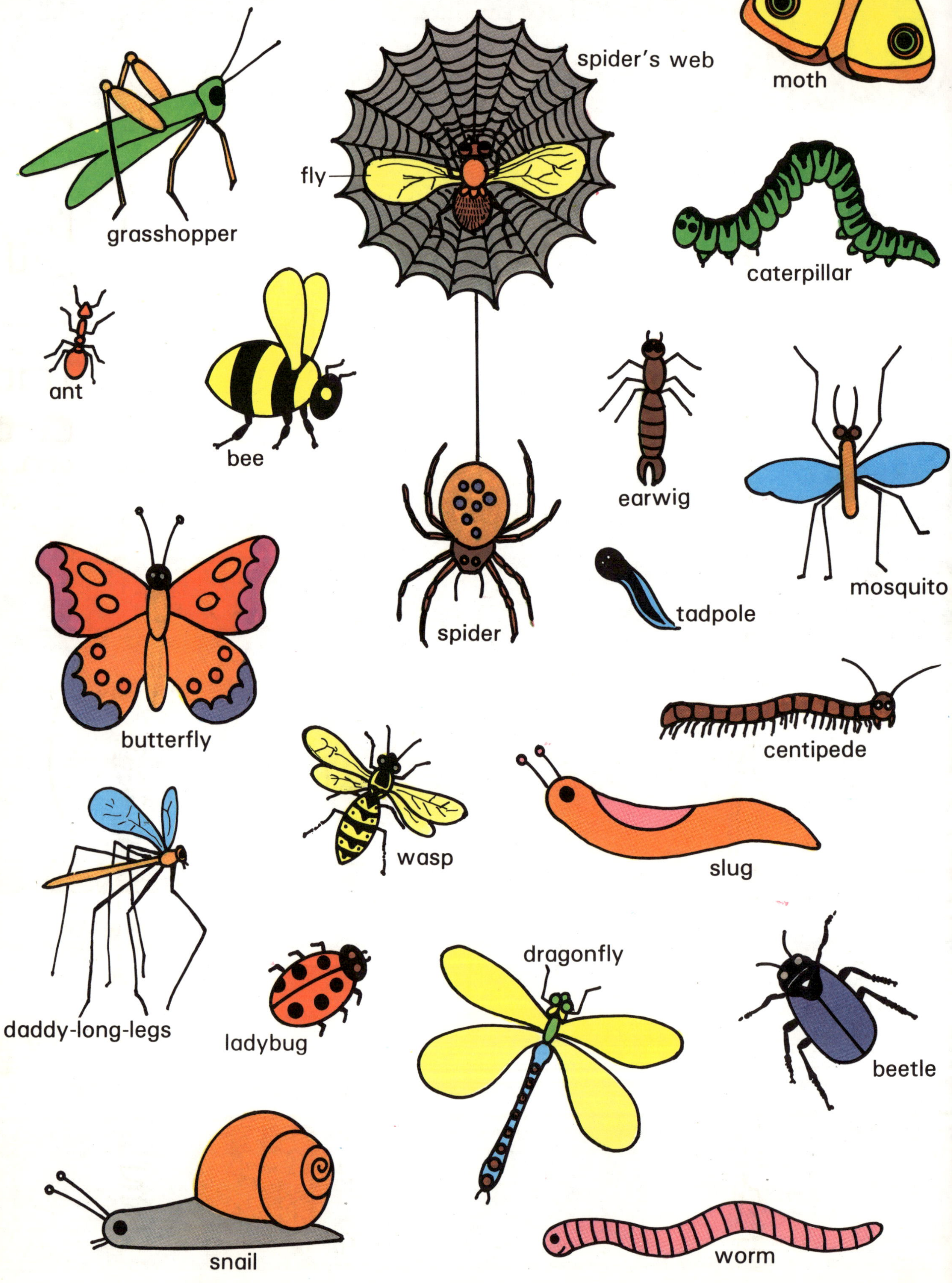

Flowers

sunflower
foxglove
dahlia
rose
snowdrop
daffodil
lupin
tulip
pansy
crocus
poppy
bluebell
dandelion
daisy
violet
buttercup
forget-me-not

Pets

dog
puppy
macaw
hamster
pony
rabbit
mouse
gerbil
guinea pig
tortoise/turtle
goldfish
kitten
cat

Birds

rooster
chick
hen
duck
duckling
turkey
goose
swallow
sparrow
gosling
crow
robin
bluebird
blackbird
pigeon
thrush
starling
wren
owl
swan
cygnet
flamingo
eagle

2 Numbers

one elephant

two cars

three fish

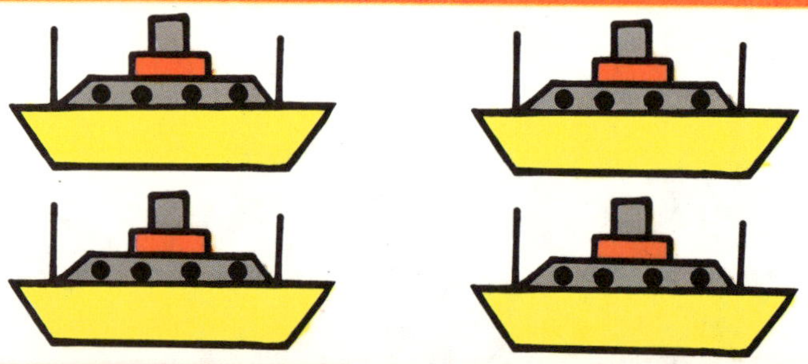

four ships

five drums

six toadstools

seven apples

eight birds

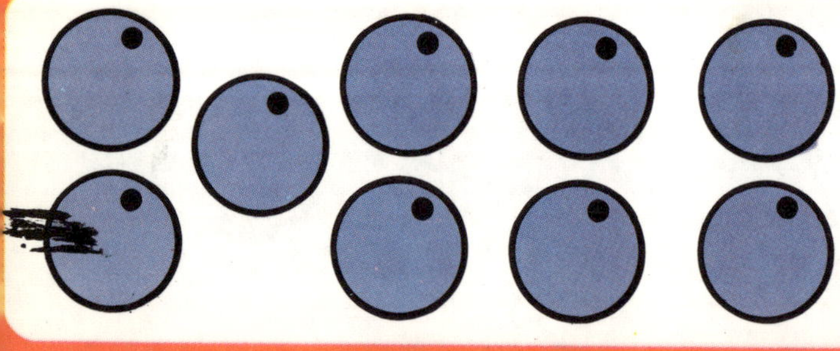

nine beads

ten ants

Shapes and colors

orange circle

black star

yellow square

purple diamond

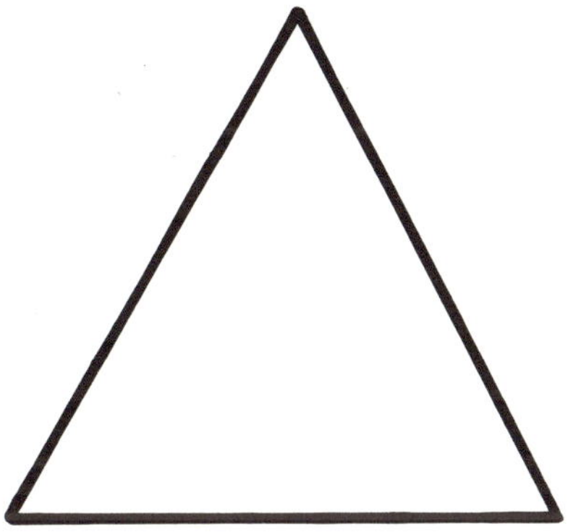

white triangle

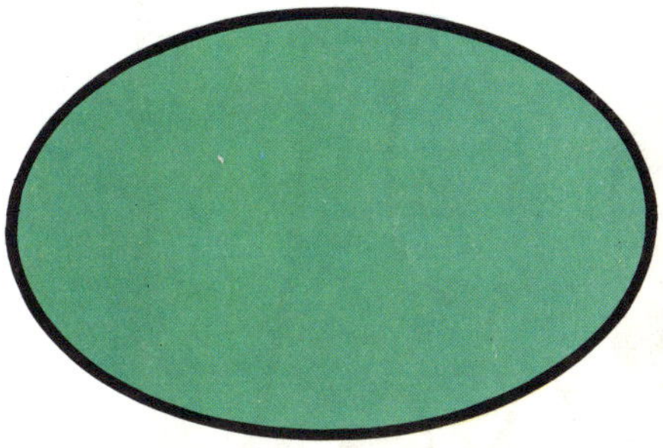

turquoise oval

brown cone

red rectangle

pink cube

green pyramid

blue heart

grey cylinder

Days of the week

Monday

Monday's child is fair of face

Tuesday

Tuesday's child is full of grace

Wednesday

Wednesday's child is full of woe

Thursday

Thursday's child has far to go

Friday

Friday's child is loving and giving

Saturday

Saturday's child works hard for a living

Sunday

but the child that is born on the Sabbath day is bonny and blithe and good and gay

Times of day

quarter to seven

dawn – sunrise

time to get up

eight o'clock

morning

time for breakfast

twelve o'clock

midday

time for lunch/dinner

half past three

afternoon

time for snacks

six o'clock

dusk – evening

time for supper

quarter past eight

night

time for bed

Months of the year

January
February
March
April
May
June
July
August
September
October
November
December

Seasons

Some places have four seasons

spring

summer

autumn

winter

Some places have two seasons

wet season

dry season

Weather

cloud

sun

rain

wind

snow and ice

frost

thunder and lightning

fog

PRINTED IN BELGIUM BY
proost
INTERNATIONAL BOOK PRODUCTION